ASL (American Sign Language) Alphabet & Tracing Workbook

Early Learning • Handwriting • ASL Communication Skills

By Jermiko Thomas

National & International Award-Winning Author

Educational Market Best-Selling Author

Cornhill Publishing

This Workbook Belongs To:

_____(Write Your Name)

Table of Contents

- How to Use This Workbook

- ASL Alphabet Chart (A–Z)

- ASL Numbers Chart (1–20)

- Letters A- Z ASL Worksheet

- Number & Tracing (1–20)ASL Worksheet

How to Use This Workbook

The ASL Alphabet & Tracing Workbook is designed to help children build early communication skills through American Sign Language while strengthening handwriting and fine motor development.

Recommended Use:

- 5–10 minutes per day
- Introduce 1–2 letters per session
- Model the ASL handshape before tracing
- Encourage students to: say the letter, sign the letter, trace the letter, color the handshape

Skill Areas Supported:

- Alphabet mastery
- ASL awareness and early signing
- Handwriting and fine motor skills
- Confidence-building for emerging communicators
- Inclusive learning and empathy

ASL Alphabet Chart (A–Z)

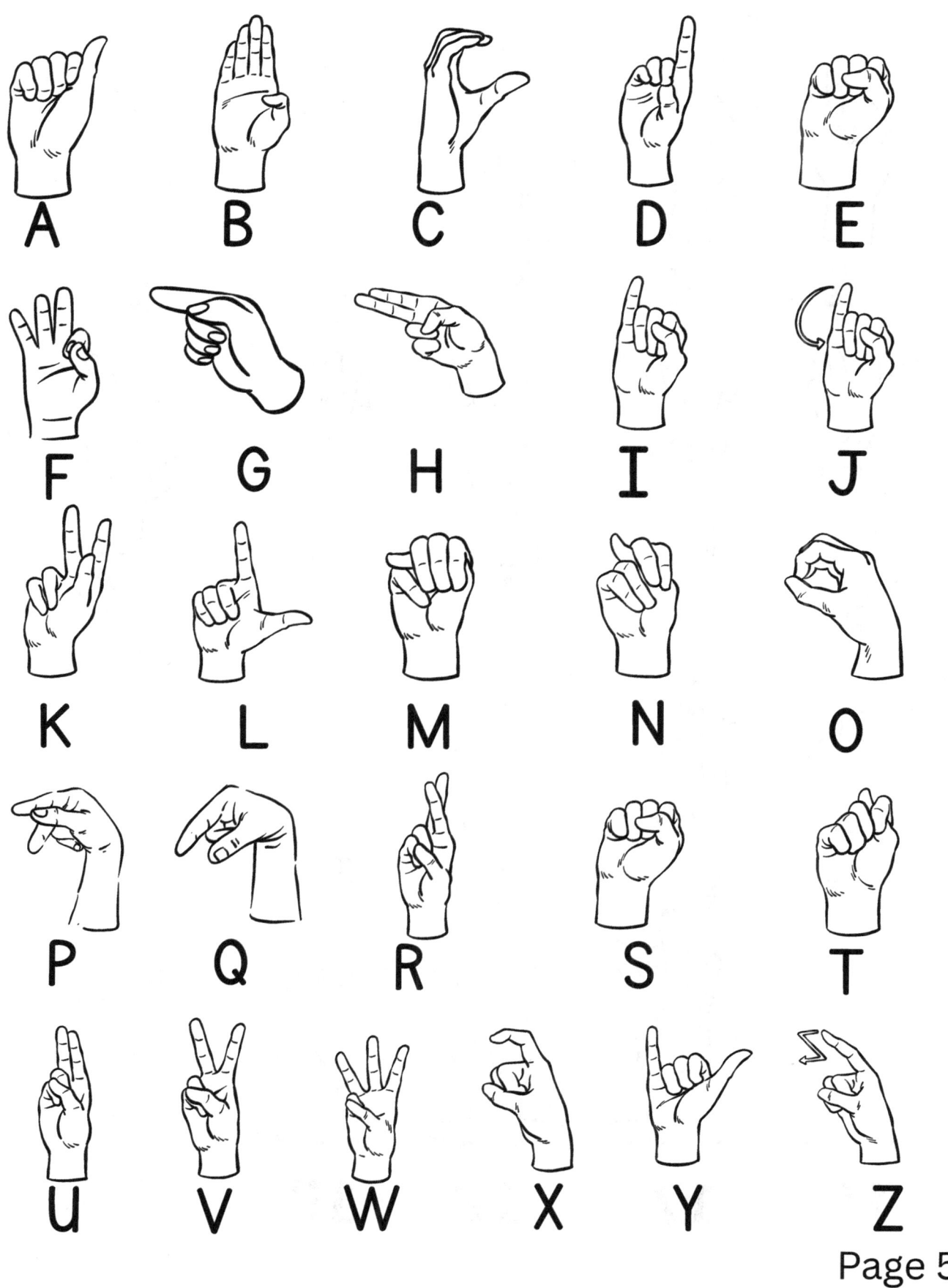

Page 5

ASL Numbers Chart (1-20)

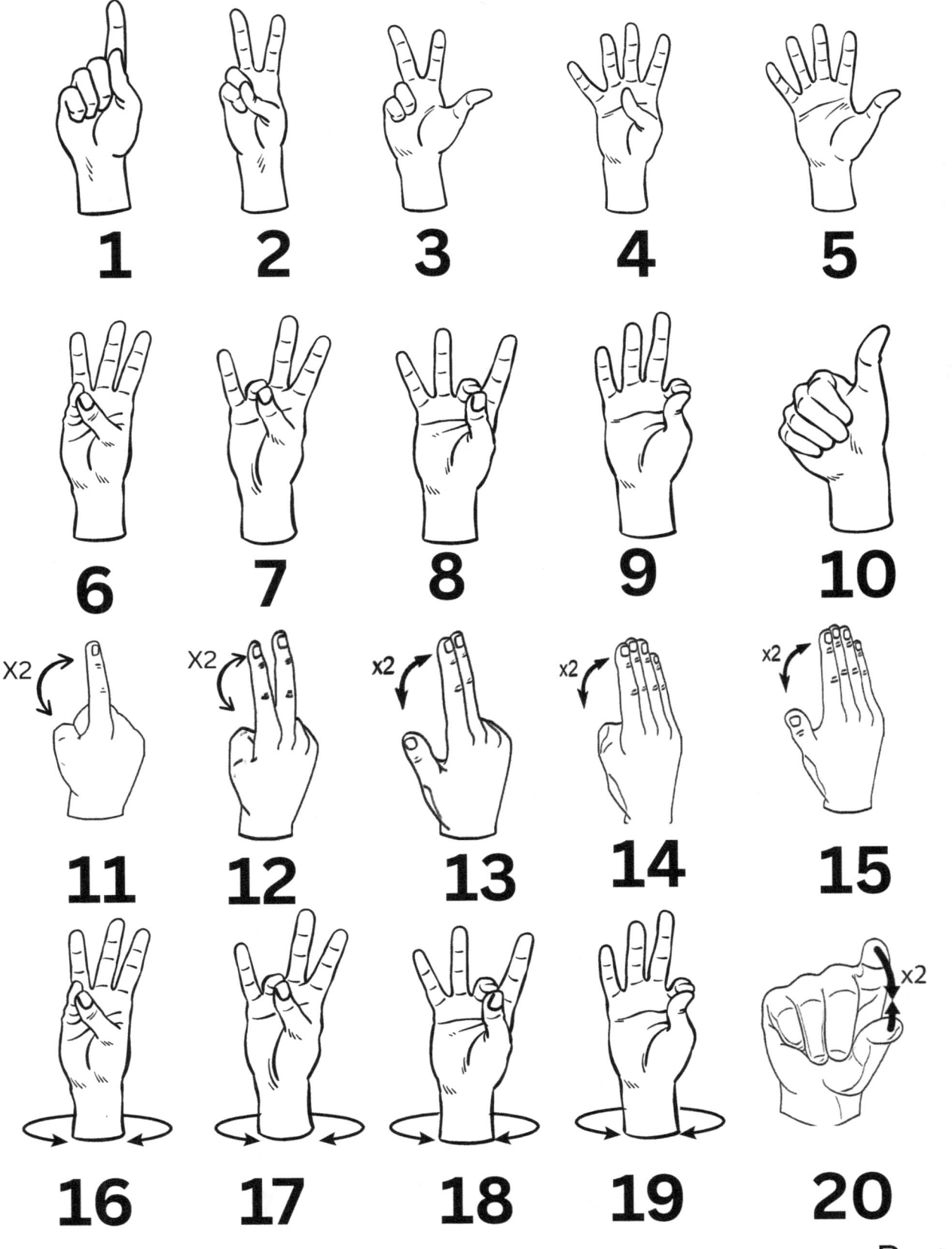

Name: _____ Date: _____

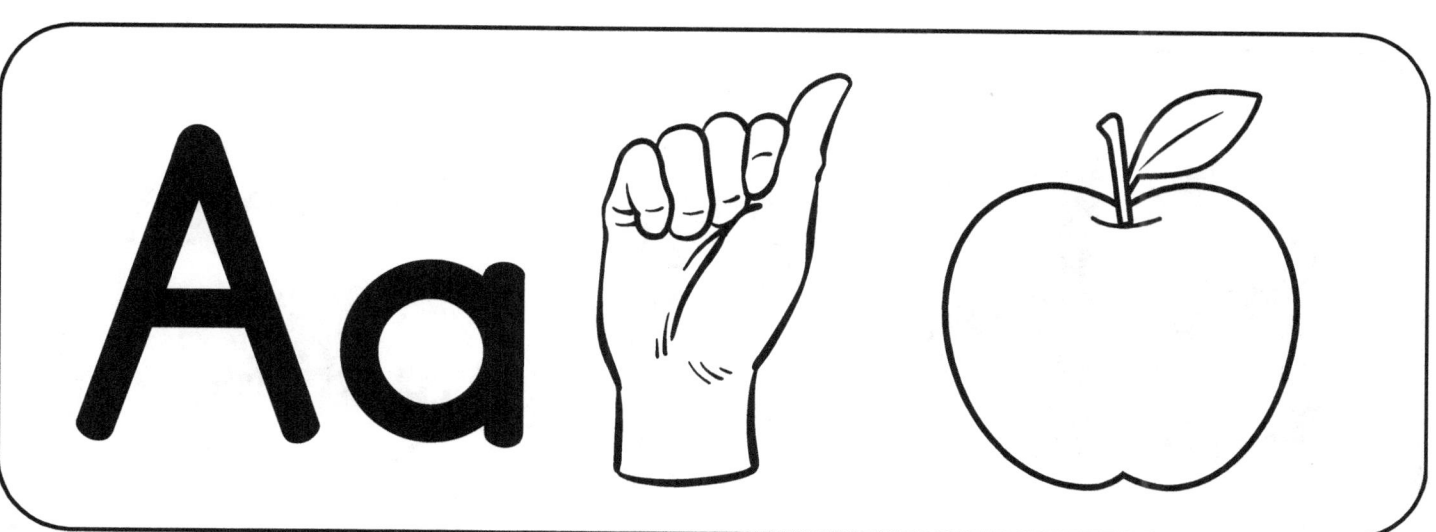

Trace the letters.

Page 7

Name: _____ Date: _____

Bb

Trace the letters.

B B B B B B
B B B B B B
B B B B B B
B B B B B B
B B B B B B

Page 8

Name: _____ Date: _____

C c

Trace the letters.

C C C C C C
C C C C C C
C C C C C C
C C C C C C
C C C C C C

Page 9

Name: _____ Date: _____

Trace the letters.

Page 10

Name: _____ Date: _____

E e

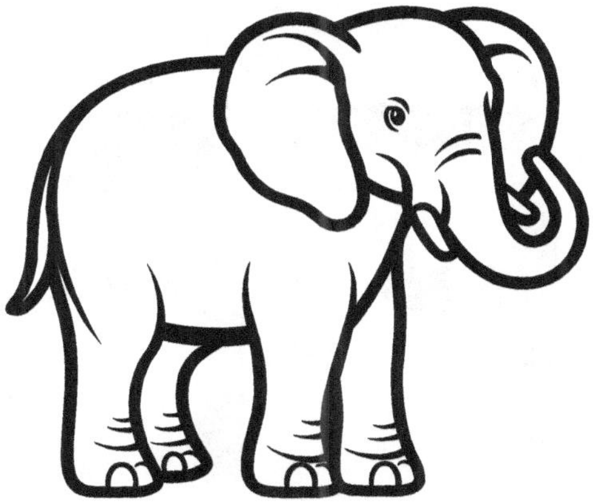

Trace the letters.

Page 11

Name: _____   Date: _____

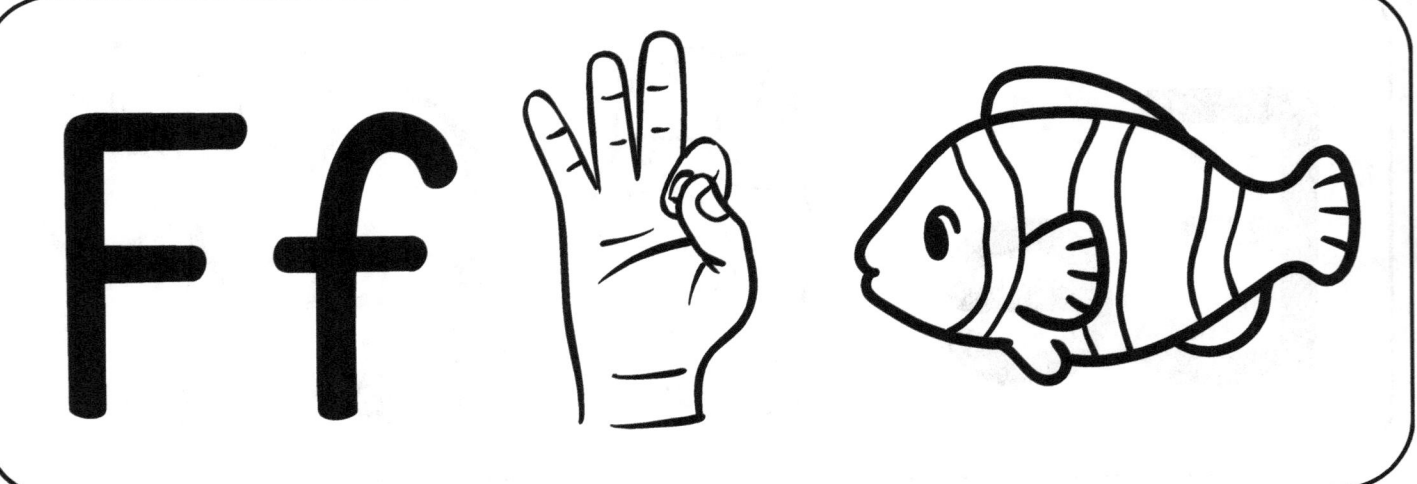

Trace the letters.

Page 12

Name: _____ Date: _____

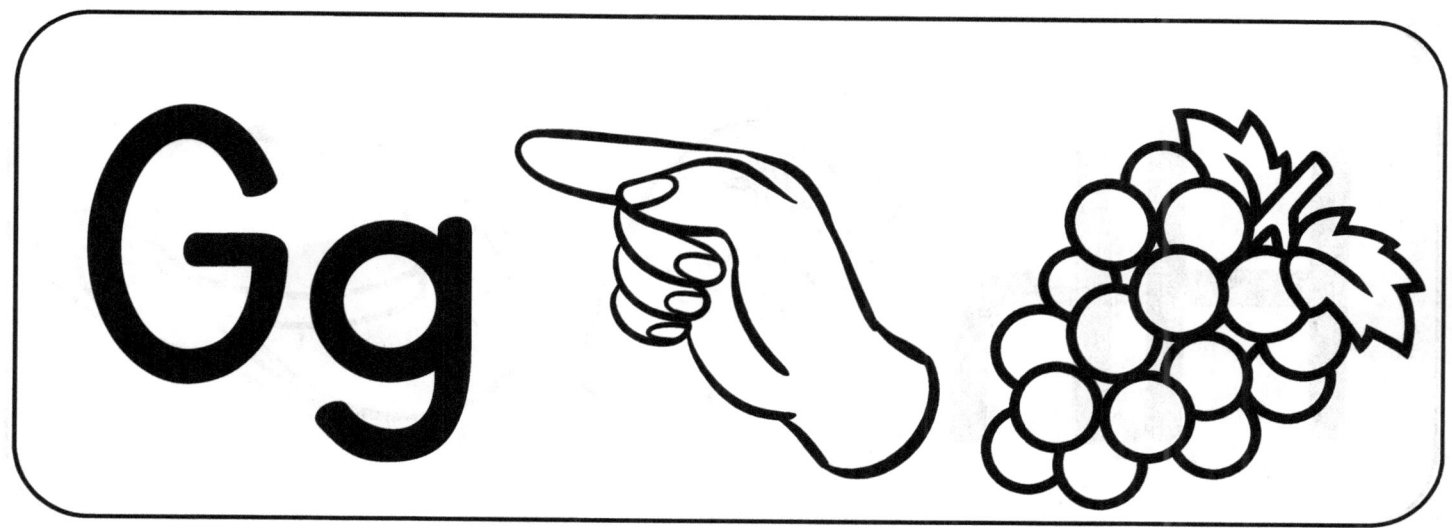

Trace the letters.

Page 13

Name: _____ Date: _____

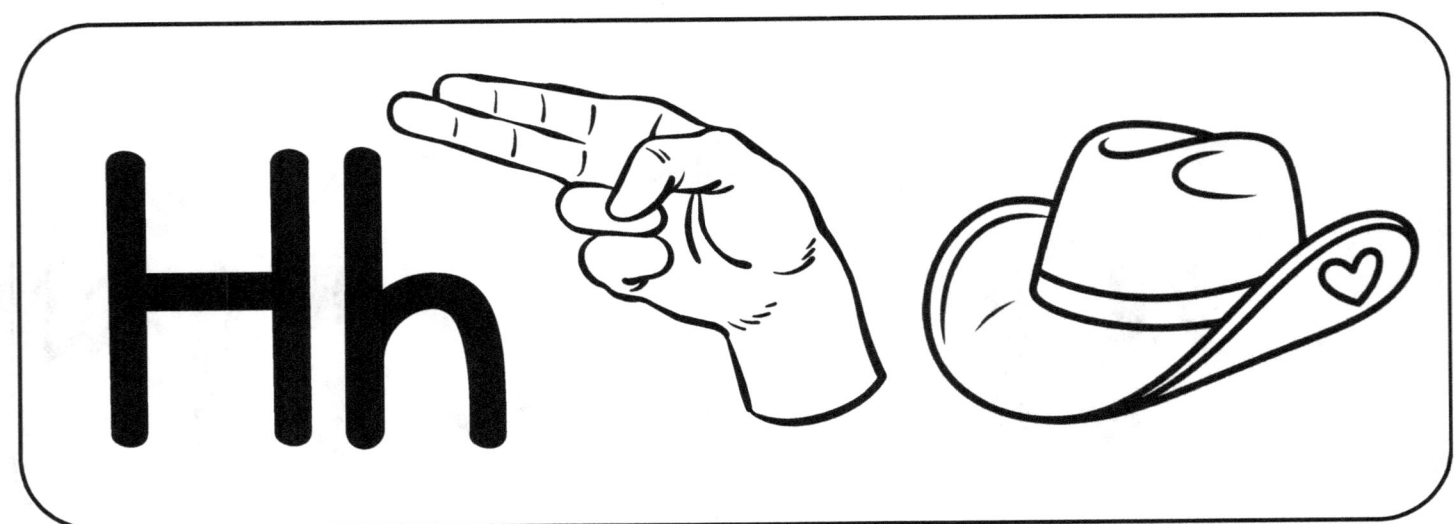

Trace the letters.

Page 14

Name: _____ Date: _____

Trace the letters.

Page 15

Name: ______________________ Date: ______________

Jj

Trace the letters.

J J J J J J

J J J J J J

J J J J J J

J J J J J J

J J J J J J

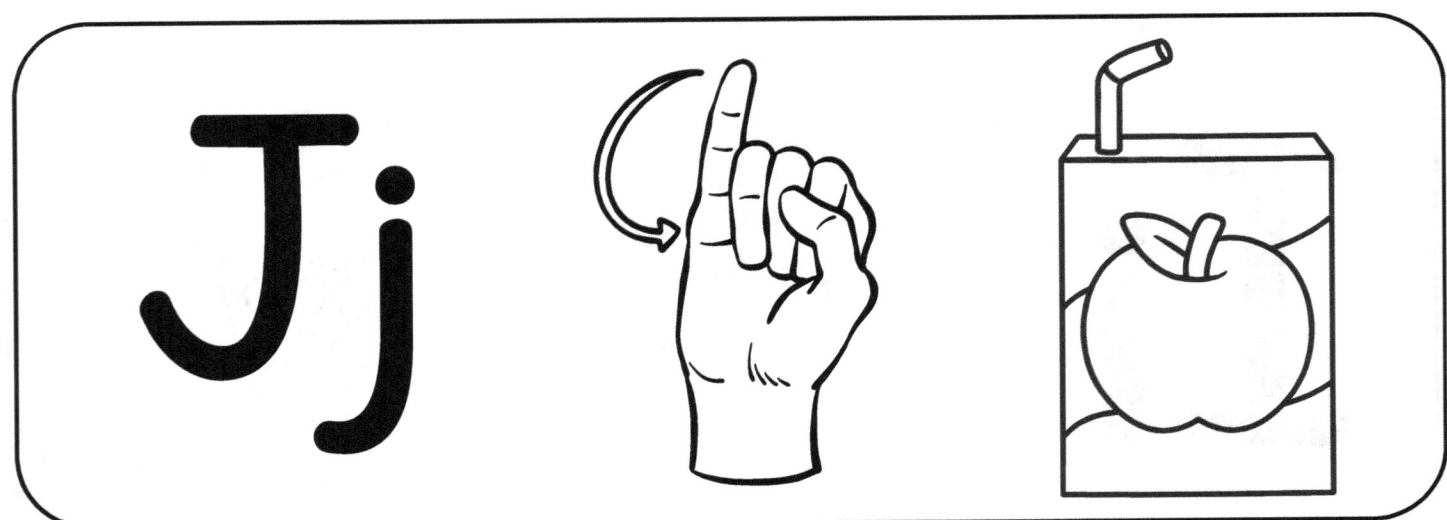

Name: _____   Date: _____

Trace the letters.

K K K K K K

K K K K K K

K K K K K K

K K K K K K

K K K K K K

Page 17

Name: _____ Date: _____

Trace the letters.

Page 18

Name: _____ Date: _____

Trace the letters.

M M M M M M

M M M M M M

M M M M M M

M M M M M M

M M M M M M

Name: ______________________ Date: ______________

Nn

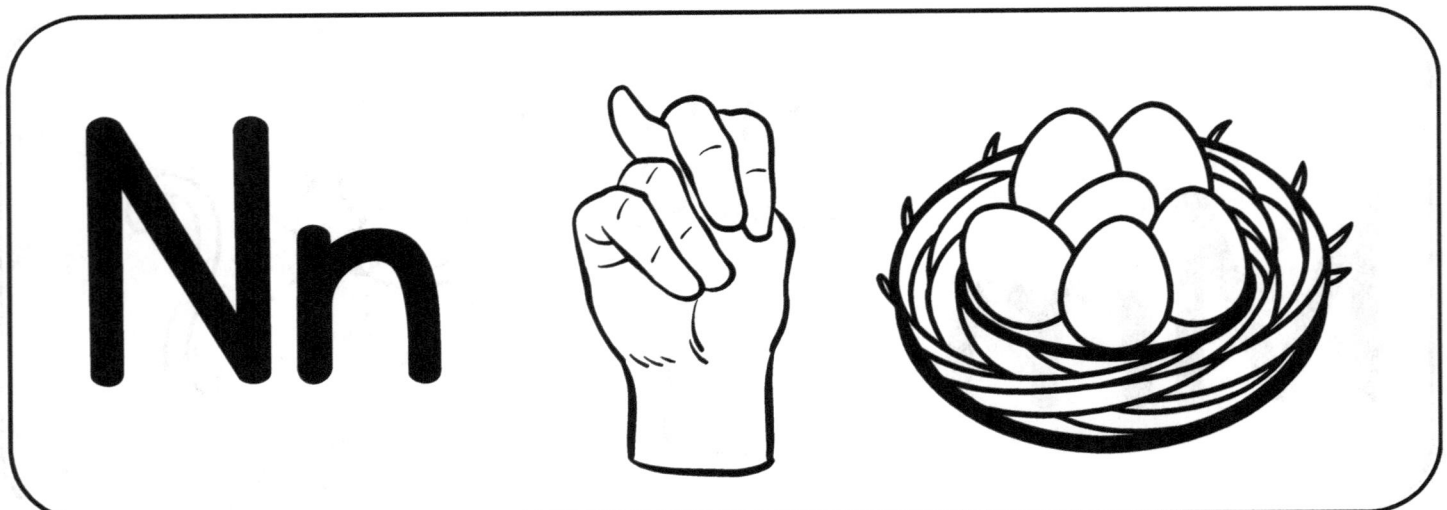

Trace the letters.

Name: _____ Date: _____

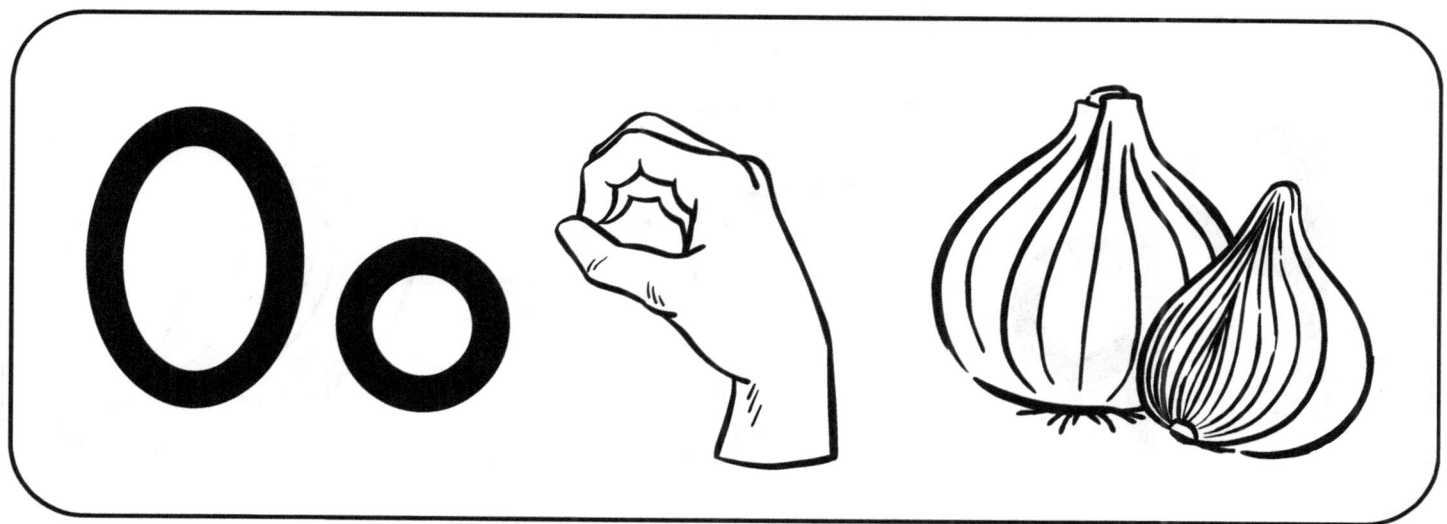

Trace the letters.

Page 21

Name: _____ Date: _____

Trace the letters.

Page 22

Name: _____ Date: _____

Trace the letters.

Name: _____ Date: _____

Trace the letters.

R R R R R R

R R R R R R

R R R R R R

R R R R R R

R R R R R R

Name: _____ Date: _____

Trace the letters.

Name: _____ Date: _____

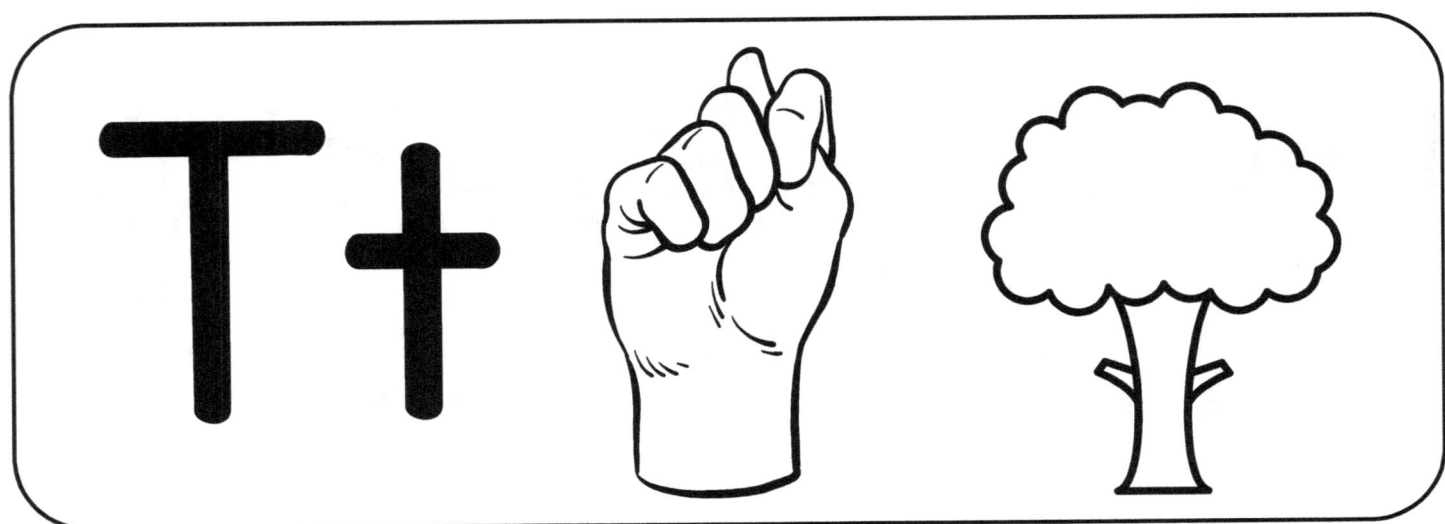

Trace the letters.

Page 26

Name: _____ Date: _____

Trace the letters.

Name: _____ Date: _____

Trace the letters.

Page 28

Name: _____ Date: _____

Trace the letters.

Name: _____ Date: _____

Trace the letters.

Name: _____ Date: _____

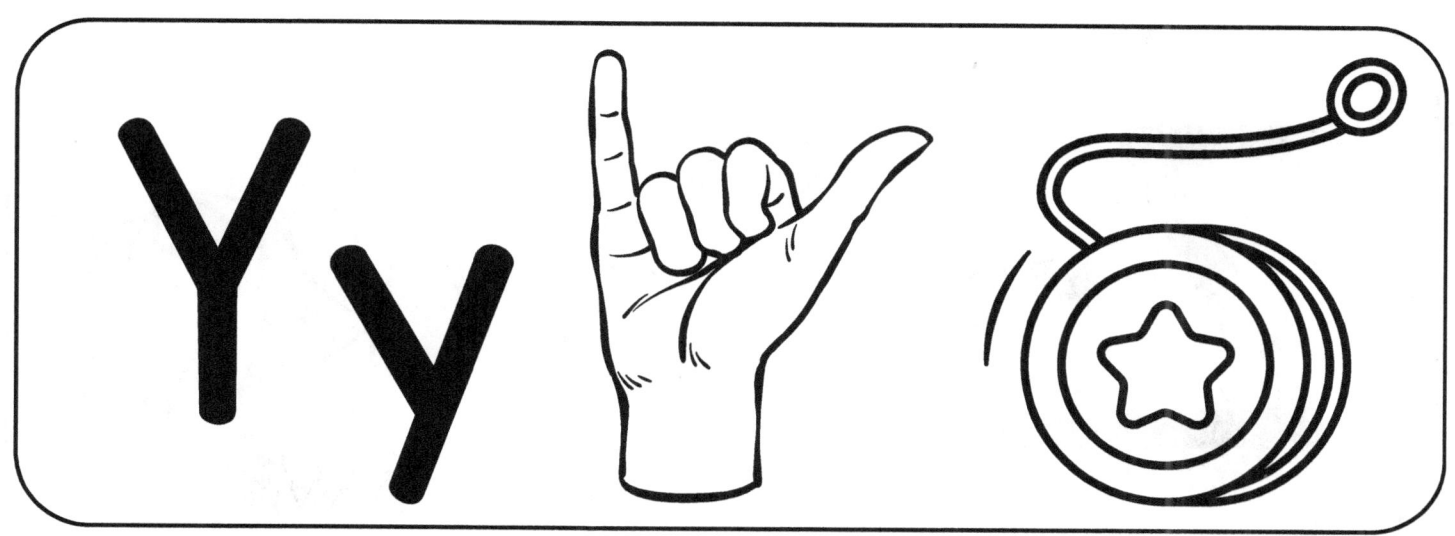

Trace the letters.

Page 31

Name: _____ Date: _____

Trace the letters.

Name: _____   Date: _____

I

Trace the letters.

Page 33

Name: _____ Date: _____

2

Trace the letters.

Page 34

Name: _____ Date: _____

3

Trace the letters.

3 — 3 — 3 — 3 — 3 — 3

3 — 3 — 3 — 3 — 3 — 3

3 — 3 — 3 — 3 — 3 — 3

3 — 3 — 3 — 3 — 3 — 3

3 — 3 — 3 — 3 — 3 — 3

Name: _____ Date: _____

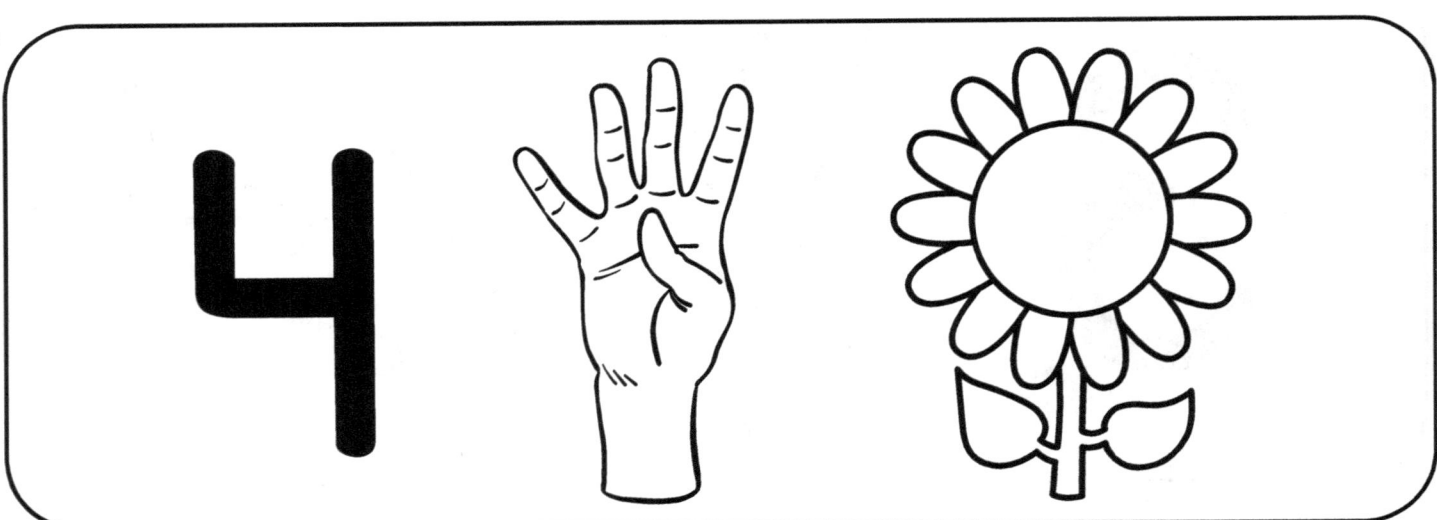

Trace the numbers.

Name: _____ Date: _____

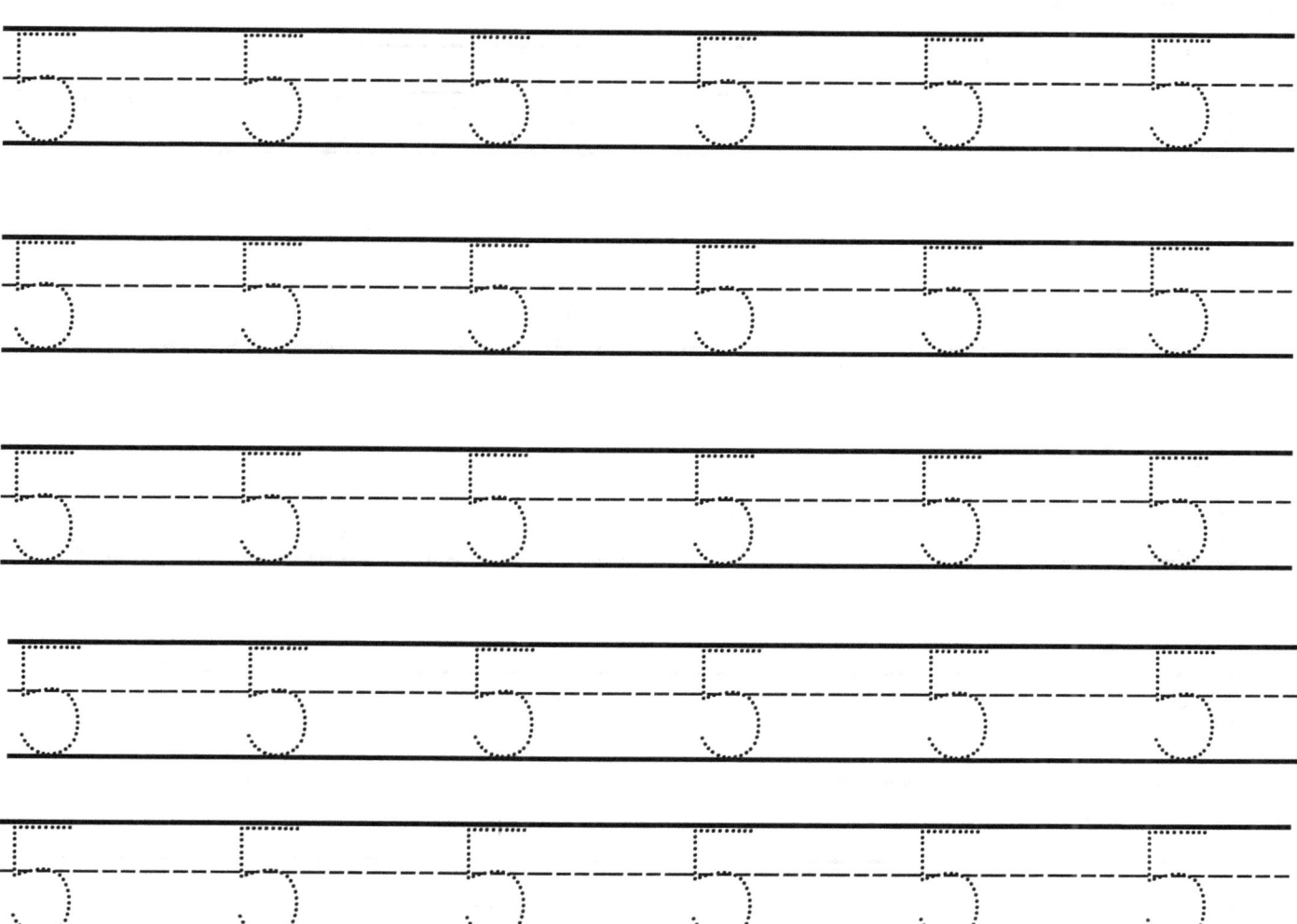

Trace the numbers.

Page 37

Name: _____ Date: _____

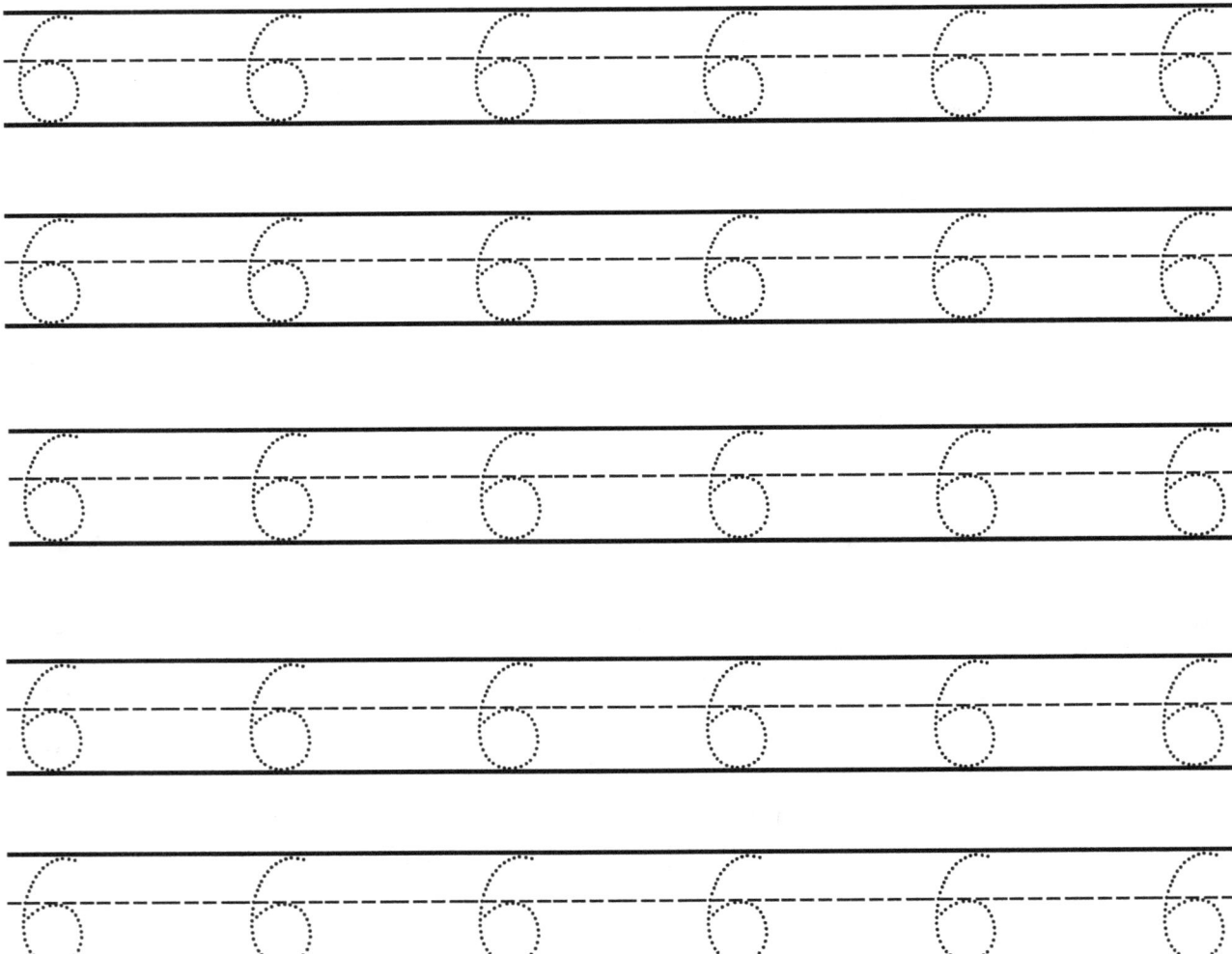

Trace the numbers.

Page 38

Name: _____ Date: _____

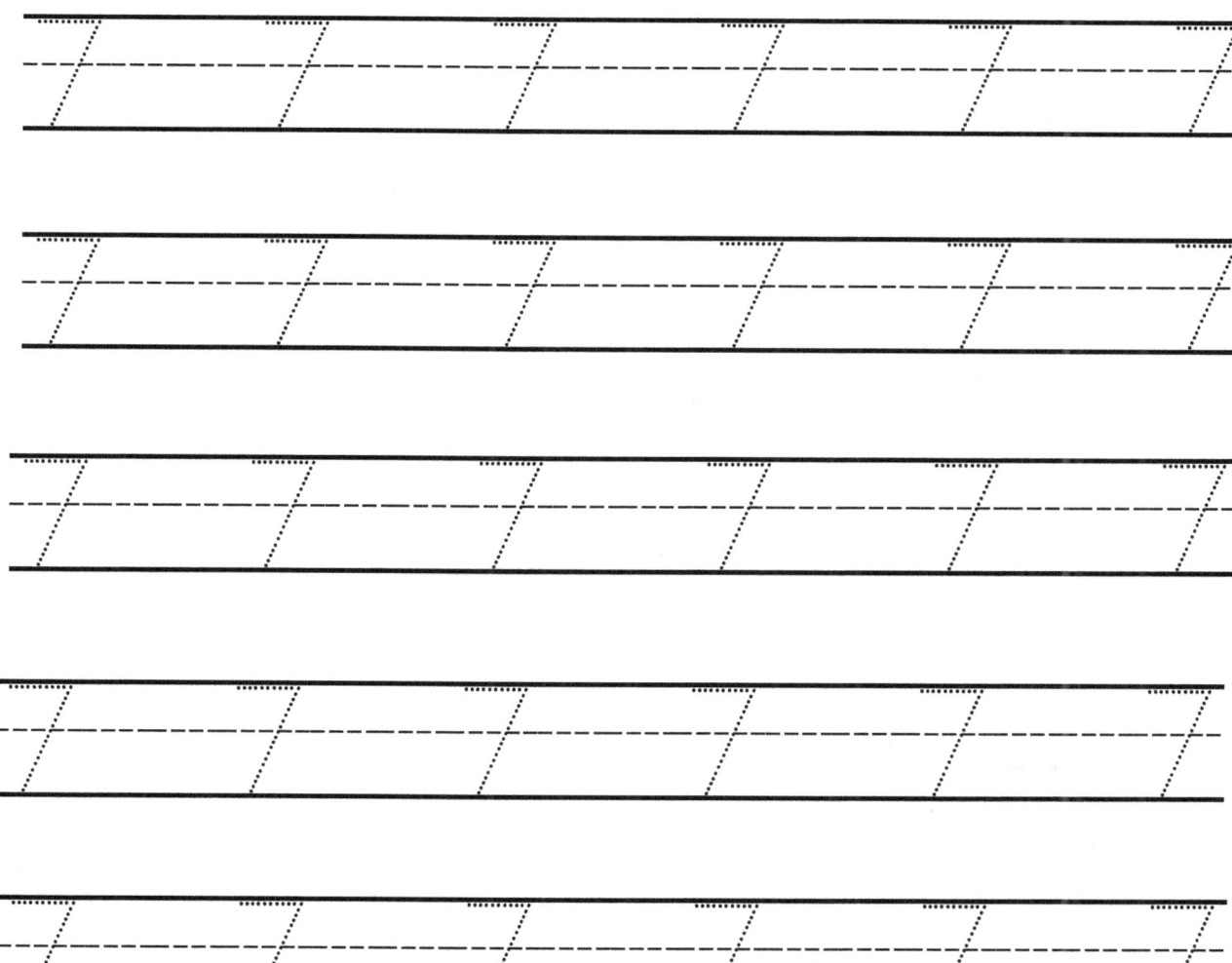

Trace the numbers.

Page 39

Name: ____________________ Date: ______________

8

Trace the numbers.

8 8 8 8 8 8

8 8 8 8 8 8

8 8 8 8 8 8

8 8 8 8 8 8

8 8 8 8 8 8

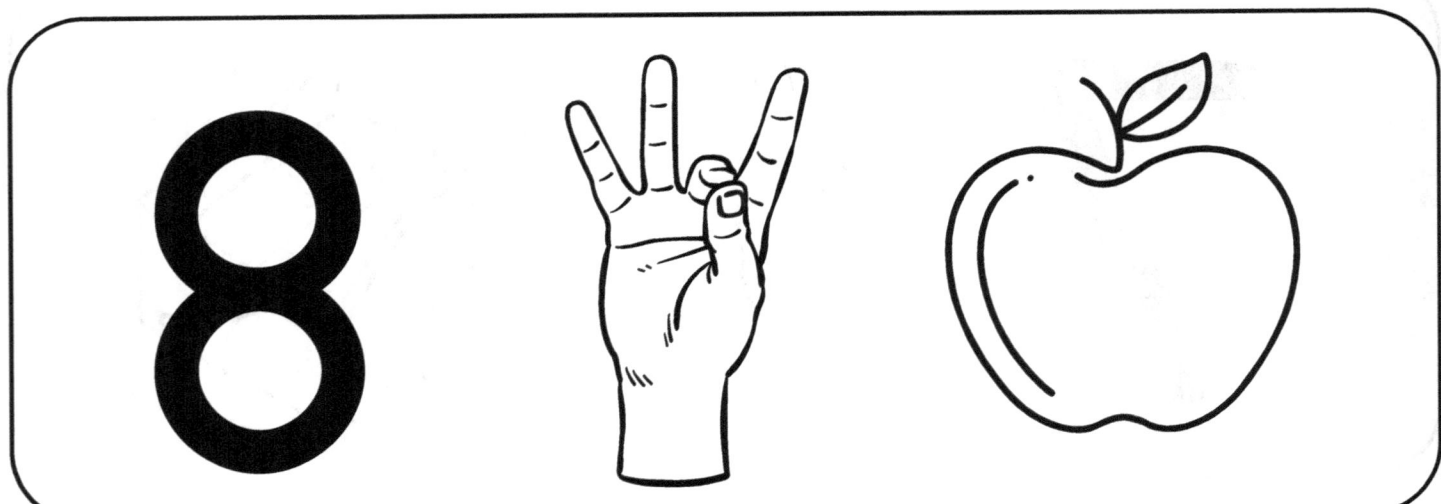

Name: _____ Date: _____

Trace the numbers.

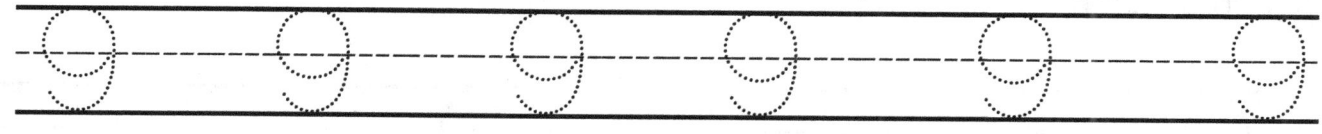

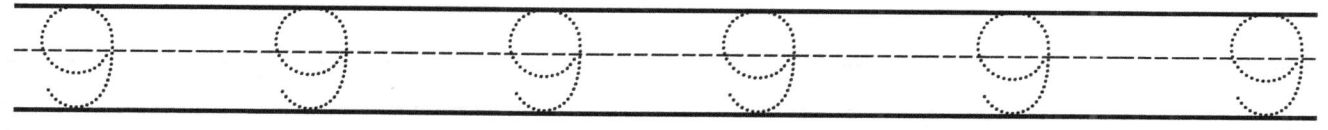

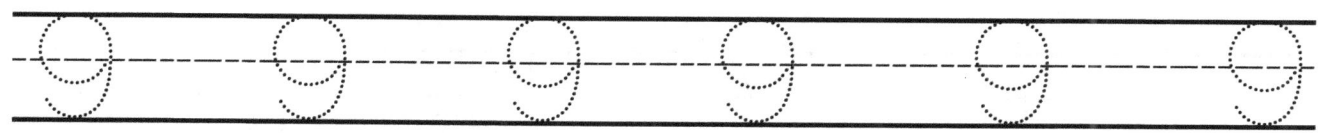

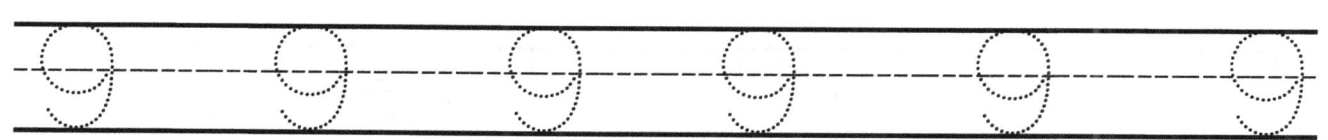

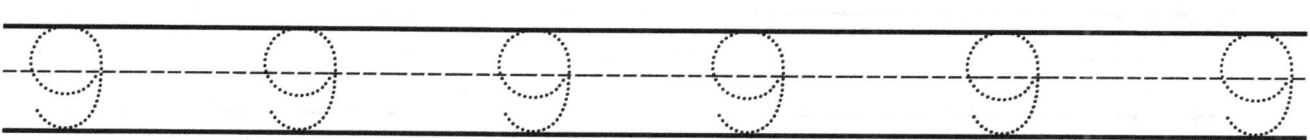

Name: _____ Date: _____

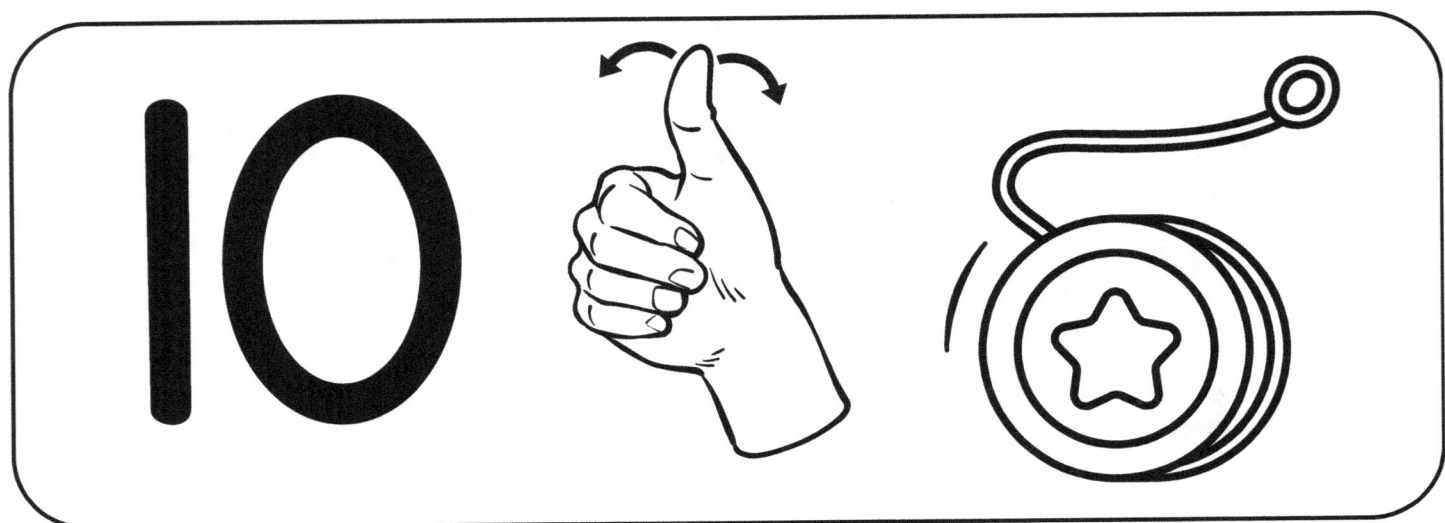

Trace the numbers.

Page 42

Name: _____ Date: _____

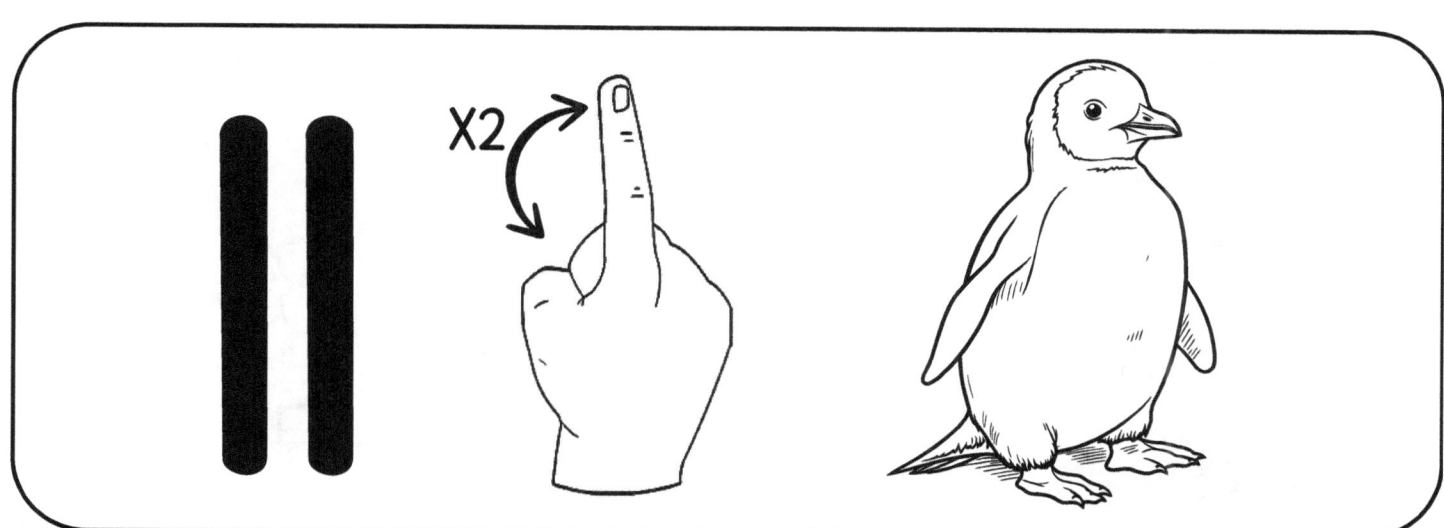

Trace the numbers.

Page 43

Name: _____ Date: _____

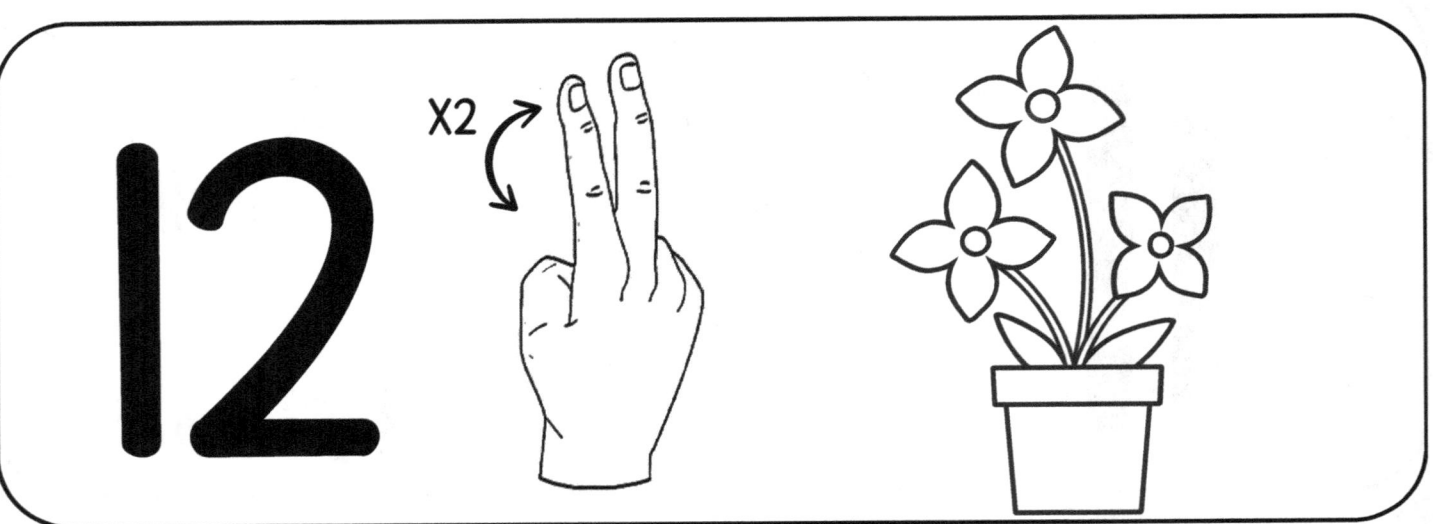

Trace the numbers.

12 12 12 12 12 12

12 12 12 12 12 12

12 12 12 12 12 12

12 12 12 12 12 12

12 12 12 12 12 12

Name: _____ Date: _____

13

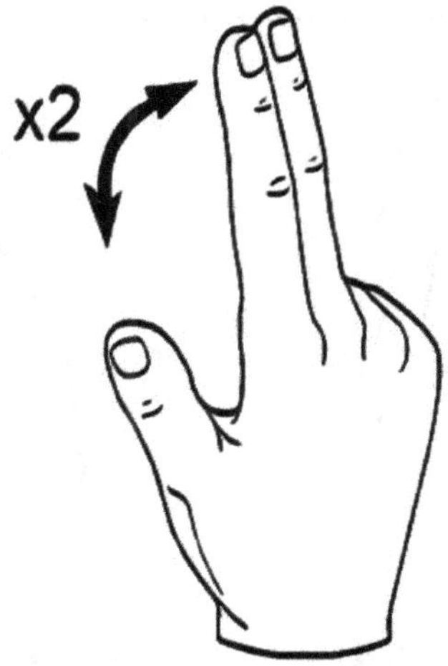

Trace the numbers.

13 — 13 — 13 — 13 — 13 — 13

13 — 13 — 13 — 13 — 13 — 13

13 — 13 — 13 — 13 — 13 — 13

13 — 13 — 13 — 13 — 13 — 13

13 — 13 — 13 — 13 — 13 — 13

Name: _____ Date: _____

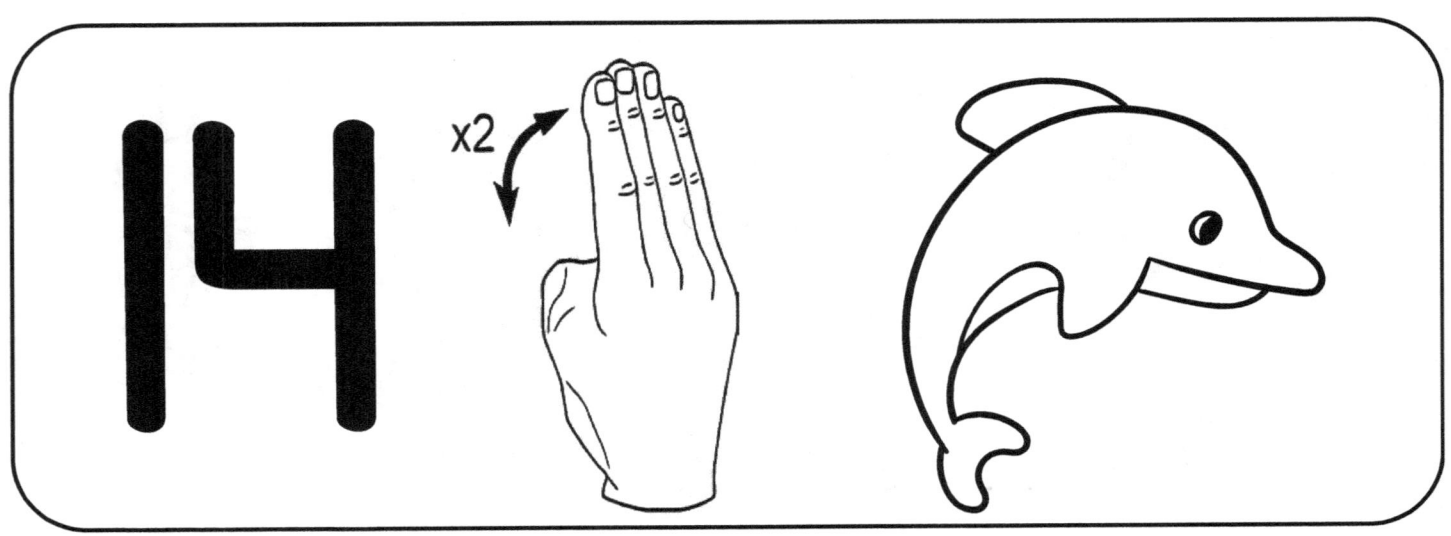

Trace the numbers.

Name: _____ Date: _____

15 x2

Trace the numbers.

15 15 15 15 15 15

15 15 15 15 15 15

15 15 15 15 15 15

15 15 15 15 15 15

15 15 15 15 15 15

Name: _____   Date: _____

Trace the numbers.

16 16 16 16 16 16

16 16 16 16 16 16

16 16 16 16 16 16

16 16 16 16 16 16

16 16 16 16 16 16

Name: _____ Date: _____

Trace the numbers.

Page 49

Name: _____ Date: _____

Trace the numbers.

18 18 18 18 18 18

18 18 18 18 18 18

18 18 18 18 18 18

18 18 18 18 18 18

18 18 18 18 18 18

Name: _____ Date: _____

Trace the numbers.

Page 51

Name: _____ Date: _____

20

Trace the numbers.

20 20 20 20 20 20

20 20 20 20 20 20

20 20 20 20 20 20

20 20 20 20 20 20

20 20 20 20 20 20